c1964

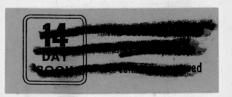

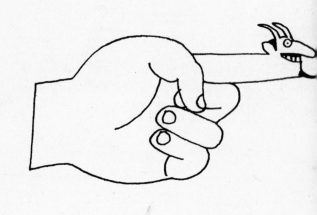

A SEIZURE OF LIMERICKS

CONRAD AIKEN

A SEIZURE OF LIMERICKS

Designer: Milton Glaser
80190-0214
Printed in the United States of America

Library of Congress Catalog Card Number: 64-21924
First Edition
Fourteen of the limericks in this volume were first published in *Horizon*.

CONTENTS

For Hy Sobiloff

a very small quid

for a very large quo.

1

The limerick's, admitted, a verse form:

a terse form: a curse form: a hearse form.

It may not be lyric,

and at best it's Satyric,

and a whale of a tail in perverse form.

2

There once was a wicked young minister

whose conduct was thought to be sinister.

By ruses nightmarish

he seduced the whole parish

except for one squeamish old spinister.

3

Said a dreadfully literate cat

I've had my Litt. D and all that.

And in New York, my dear,

when I read "Litter Here",

why I litter at once and then scat.

4

Said a scion of Boston society

who was pinched, and for mere inebriety,

    I will lie in this gutter

    refusing to utter

one word in defense of sobriety.

5

There was an old micky named Cassidy.

who was famed for impromptu mendacity.

When asked did he lie

he replied: to reply

would be to impugn his yeracity.

6

Quoth a cow in the marshes of Glynn

all the world is divine, even sin.

As a natural creature

I worship all nature,

but most when the bullrush is in.

7

It's time to make love: douse the glim.

The fireflies twinkle and dim.

The stars lean together

like birds of a feather

and the loin lies down with the limb.

8

Said Isolde to Tristan, how curious!

Old Mark is becoming quite furious.

Since we got off that boat

it's been all Liebestod:

is it possible Wagner is spurious?

9

Said the Reverend S. McCord Crothers,

my very dear sisters and brothers

we are met, are we not,

to hear what I forgot

to tell Crothers to tell to the others.

10

I'm bored, said a right-angled triangle.

Fed up with this rectitude angle.

And what *is* the use

of a hypotenuse

if she hasn't got bangs and a bangle?

11

Said a lovely Greek maiden named Clytie

I look mighty nice in my nightie:

    but beyond all   compare

    I look cuter   when bare,

and when I am bare   I am bitey.

12

Farewell to the dear days of Genesis.

We do these thing now all by synthesis.

    And who would not rather

    have a test-tube for father

than a *homo in loco* *parenthesis?*

13

Said a point being approached by a locus:

I consider this sheer hocus-pocus.

What good will it do me

if it never gets to me?

Will someone please tell it to *focus?*

14

Tired of the quarrel with self I

toild up to that high mountain shelf: I

gazed down at a world

where no self lay furled

and rejoiced to hear no voice from Delphi.

15

A giddy young lass of Sesuit

fell in love with a lad from Cotuit;

said the preacher from Wareham

who proceeded to pair 'em,

Sesuit, cotuit, go to it.

16

One umbilical cord to another:

I presume that of course you're my brother.

 And as we are twins

 and nobody wins

I suggest we just stay here in Mother.

17

I'm an aesthete, I don't wash my neck.

As for sex, why I just hunt and peck.

Who cares about gender

provided it's tender

and *you're* the too Touleuse-Lautrec?

18

Said an Ogre from old Saratoga

I've tried to de-Ogre by Yoga

    I've stood on my head

    all day in my bed

but the mirror still says I'm an Ogre.

19

Whether or not said by old Thoreau

it is wiser to beg than to borrow.

How true that at any rate

and even a penny rate

to borrow tomorrow means sorrow.

20

I don't give a hoot said a particle

if I can't have the definite article.

    If *cogito sum*

    pronounces my doom

to hell with all systems Descartesical.

21

Said a much-travelled wench from Virginia

who cares about far Abyssinia?

　　And if　even Selassie

　　should　make you his lassie

it still would　depend on what's in you.

22

A delectable gal from Augusta

vowed that nobody ever had bussed her.

But an expert from France

took a bilingual chance

and the mixture of tongues quite nonplused her

23

Animula vagula blandula,

is it true that your origin's glandular?

Must you twang for the Lord

an umbilical chord

like all other impropagandula?

24

Said the God-maker Judas Iscariot

as he flung to the tree-top his lariat

pray bear me, dear tree,

till the days number three,

and Time cuts me down for his chariot.

25

Neighed an oyster-fed stallion from Whitstable

I think it's high time that I quit stable:

and without asking pardon

I will just follow hard on

the first little filly to flit stable.

26

Nan, Saw, and Paw, of Setucket,

between them had only one bucket:

Nan took it and ran

and the trouble began:

Sawtucket, Pawtucket, Nantucket.

27

Great archers and hitters of bull's-eyes,

you wingers of wren's eyes and gulls' eyes,

Ulysses and Tell

and Achilles as well,

where walk you now baring your skull's eyes?

28

What is truth said the cynical Pilate

that ignorant men should defile it?

From the source to the seed

all nature's agreed,

it is only man's mind would restyle it.

29

I'm the loin of Babylon town

I'm the lion what ain't loin down:

   Good-bye, obelisk,

     farewell, odalisque,

I'm the loin what ain't lion down.

30

Said a gal who disdained Willimantic

my boyfriend I fear's too romantic

he becomes simply frantic

if I am too antic

with the male population of Yantic.

31

There once was a wonderful wizard

who got a fierce pain in his gizzard

so he drank wind and snow

at fifty below

and farted a forty-day blizzard.

32

A much-too-plump damsel of Chatham

was afflicted alas with a fat ham.

she tried and she tried

but it can't be denied

that she seldom had mustard on *that* ham.

33

An uxorious female named Emily

longed for years to be Jupiter's Semele

She had to make do

with a pawnbroker Jew

but by Jove she achieved quite a femeleh

34

With the critical Randall Jarrell

few poets presume to quarrell

    so they hate and they hate

      while they wait and they wait

to put him across a barrell.

35

Sighed a dear little shipboard divinity

in a deckchair I lost my virginity

    I was glancing to leeward

      when along came a steward

and undid my belief in the trinity.

36

Said a curve I'm becoming hysterical

it is hell to be merely numerical

I bend and I bend

but where will I end

in a world that is hopelessly spherical?

37

I'm a water-witch moistly incurable

wept old Anna Liffey the plurabelle

come Golden Gate span

be my arch angel man

and as lengthy and strengthy and durable.

38

Said a cool little miss from Schenectady

a murrein on words like synechdoche

let some master of arts

play with wholes and with parts

as for me I prefer hysterectomy.

39

A buttocky beauty named Bella

went out for a ride with a fella

    they returned from the ride

    with nothing outside

but the knob of the fella's umbrella.

40

Said a Parisienne of the *highlife*

how boring is life with a figleaf

    let us hie to the Louvre

    and from every *chef d'oeuvre*

remove with a chisel the big leaf.

41

The movie star queen Theda Bara

was born in the desert Sahara:

    it was, was it not,

    the Oasis of Tuat–?

and what, might we ask, could be fairer?

42

Said a French maiden *Je suis trop tendre*

vis-a-vis with the opposite *genre:*

    but some day mayhap

    I will find a nice chap

who'll instruct me in double-entendre.

43

On the deck of a ship called the Masm

an old salt was having a spasm

    cried a lady named Chasm

    is that an orgasm?

And the old salt replied to her, Yas'm.

44

Said an Eskimo missie named Big Loo

little man won't you come to my igloo?

The little man ran

all the way to Japan

at the bare thought of having to dig Loo

45

Murmured saty-saint George Santayana

Freud took a long road to Nirvana

but I'll follow the wraith

of an animal faith

to the *p* in the sky of mañana.

46

Said a ruined old roué of Barnstable

I believe it entirely demonstrable

    that no matter how shaped

    any gal can be raped

provided you deal with a constable.

47

Said old Father William I'm humble

and getting too old for a tumble

    but produce me a blonde

    and I'm still not beyond

an attempt at an interesting fumble.

48

If you've got enough cash to see Venice on

hire a Grand Canal gal as your benison

but after you fondle her

on the poop of the gondola

remember to lay a few pennies on.

49

Don't put too much trust in that cortisone

and don't ever apply to the naughty zone:

   when   all else is lost

   preserve at all cost

from cortisone the naughty   old bawdy zone.

50

Mourned a limerick written by Aiken

sometimes when at night I awaken

    and think but for Lear

    I wouldn't be here

O how by that thought I am shaken!

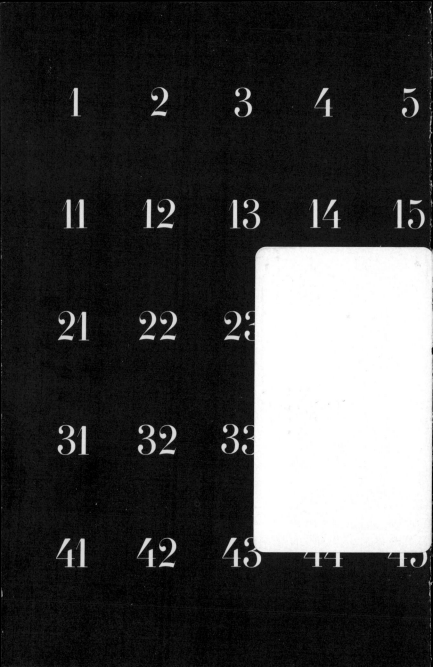